WHY IS THE AIR DIRTY?

BY ISAAC ASIMOV

Gareth Stevens Children's Books
MILWAUKEE

For a free color catalog describing Gareth Stevens' list of high-quality children's books, call 1-800-341-3569 (USA) or 1-800-461-9120 (Canada).

Library of Congress Cataloging-in-Publication Data

Asimov, Isaac, 1920-
    Why is the air dirty? / by Isaac Asimov. — A Gareth Stevens Children's Books ed.
       p. cm. — (Ask Isaac Asimov)
    Includes bibliographical references and index.
    Summary: A simple discussion of the causes and effects of air pollution and some ways
to help prevent it.
    ISBN 0-8368-0743-X
    1. Air—Pollution—Juvenile literature. 2. Air quality management—Juvenile literature.
  [1. Air—Pollution. 2. Pollution.] I. Title. II. Series: Asimov, Isaac, 1920- Ask Isaac Asimov.
  TD883.13.A85 1991
  363.73'92—dc20

                 91-50360

A Gareth Stevens Children's Books edition

Edited, designed, and produced by
Gareth Stevens Children's Books
1555 North RiverCenter Drive, Suite 201
Milwaukee, Wisconsin 53212, USA

Picture Credits
pp. 2-3, © J. G. Fuller/Hutchison Library; pp. 4-5, © Mark Cator/IMPACT Photos; pp. 6-7, Mark Mille/DeWalt and Associates, 1991; pp. 8-9, © Steve Kaufman/Bruce Coleman Limited; pp. 10-11, Rick Karpinski/DeWalt and Associates, 1991; pp. 12-13, © Nicholas De Vore/Bruce Coleman Limited; pp. 14-15, © Udo Hirsch/Bruce Coleman Limited; pp. 16-17, courtesy of NASA; pp. 18-19, © 1992 Greg Vaughn; pp. 20-21, © J. G. Fuller/Hutchison Library; pp. 22-23, © Keith Gunnar/Bruce Coleman Limited; p. 24, © Keith Gunnar/Bruce Coleman Limited

Cover photograph, © Don W. Fawcett/Visuals Unlimited: Air pollution is a problem all over the world. Smoke from a container factory spews into the air, creating a plume of pollution that can be seen for miles.

Series editor: Elizabeth Kaplan
Series designer: Sabine Beaupré
Picture researcher: Diane Laska
Consulting editor: Matthew Groshek

Printed in MEXICO

1 2 3 4 5 6 7 8 9 98 97 96 95 94 93 92

Contents

Words that appear in the glossary are printed in **boldface** type the first time they occur in the text.

Winston

Exploring Our Environment

Look around you. You see forests, fields, lakes, and rivers. You see farms, factories, houses, and cities. All of these things make up our **environment**. Sometimes there are problems with the environment. For instance, in many places the air we breathe is polluted. It often looks dirty and sometimes even smells bad. Why is the air dirty? How does dirty air harm us and other living things? Let's find out.

Up in the Air

The air surrounding our planet is made up of a mixture of gases. Nitrogen and oxygen are the main gases in the **atmosphere**. **Carbon dioxide** and water vapor are also present in small amounts. We cannot survive without these gases.

6

carbon dioxide

nitrogen

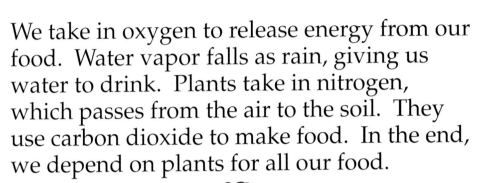

We take in oxygen to release energy from our food. Water vapor falls as rain, giving us water to drink. Plants take in nitrogen, which passes from the air to the soil. They use carbon dioxide to make food. In the end, we depend on plants for all our food.

7

oxygen

Air Pollution — Nature's Way

Gases aren't the only things floating in our atmosphere. The air naturally contains a certain amount of dirt. Erupting volcanoes spew huge amounts of dust and ash into the air. Natural forest fires and grass fires fill the air with black soot. If a large meteorite hits the Earth, the impact can send tons of dirt and rock flying into the atmosphere. The ash, dust, dirt, rock, and soot from these natural sources can darken the sky and block sunlight for months or years.

9

Air Pollution — The Human Factor

Most of the dirt in the air comes from things humans do. We throw out enormous piles of garbage that go up in smoke in huge incinerators. We burn tons of coal and oil to generate electricity. We burn natural gas in furnaces for heating. We fill the tanks of our cars with gasoline and drive millions of miles each year. Our cities and towns are choked with traffic and the air turns into a murky haze.

11

The Ugly, the Smelly, the Invisible

Burning **fossil fuels** — coal, oil, natural gas, and gasoline — releases many different pollutants into the air. We can see or smell many of these pollutants. Smoke is black with unburned carbon. Haze is brown with **nitrogen dioxide** and **hydrocarbons**. **Sulfur** gases give off a horrible smell like rotten eggs.

But some of the most dangerous pollutants are invisible. **Carbon monoxide** is released when gasoline is burned. This colorless, odorless gas can kill a person in minutes.

12

Don't Breathe the Air

Dirty air makes many people feel ill. It can make your eyes water. It can make your nose itch. It can make your throat feel scratchy and sore.

But polluted air does more than simply cause discomfort. Air pollution contributes to many different diseases. People with heart and lung problems have a harder time breathing when the air is polluted. They may have to go to the hospital if they breathe in too much polluted air. Pollutants in the air even cause some forms of cancer.

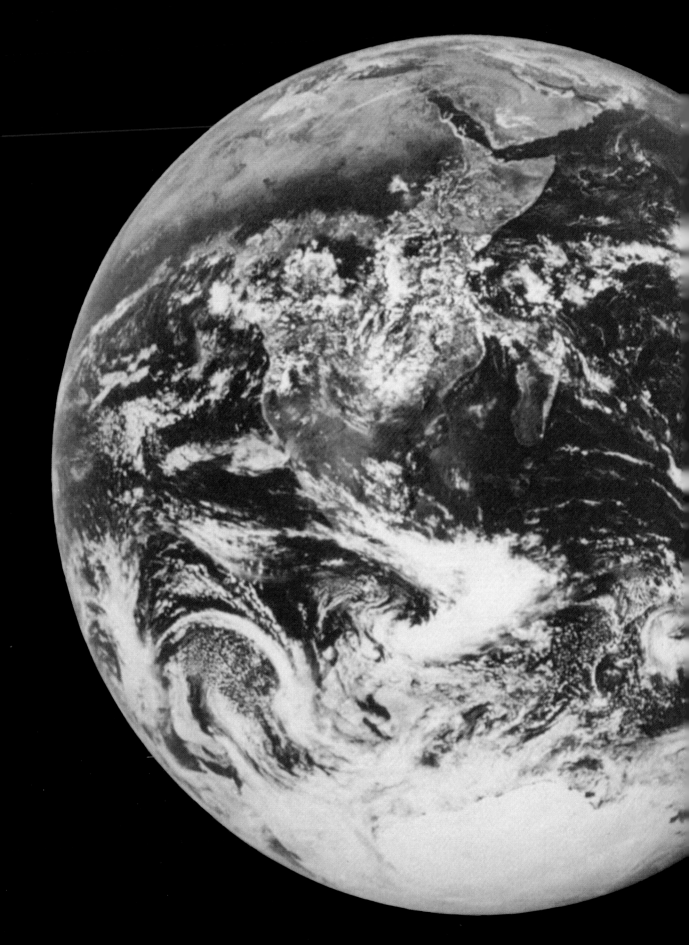

Harming the Earth

Air pollution doesn't just harm people. It can affect all life on Earth. Some pollutants, called **chlorofluorocarbons**, or CFCs, are especially dangerous. These chemicals, found in plastic-foam dishes and refrigerator coolant, actually destroy the part of our atmosphere called the ozone layer. The ozone layer helps protect the Earth from the Sun's burning rays. But CFCs are causing large holes in the ozone layer. In places near these holes, skin cancer is on the rise.

17

On a Clean-air Campaign

People have been fighting air pollution for many years. They have gotten power plants and factories to install **scrubbers** on their smokestacks. These devices clean pollutants from smoke. They have gotten car-makers to install **catalytic converters**, which remove some pollutants in car exhaust. They push for more research about forms of energy that cause little air pollution. Wind energy, generated by wind mills, as shown, is clean and safe. Solar energy is another clean alternative. Using these forms of energy can reduce levels of pollutants in the air.

The Main Culprit — the Car

Of all the things we do, driving cars causes
the most air pollution. You can help cut air
pollution by finding other ways to get
around besides in a car. You might walk
or bicycle instead of taking a ride. If you do
need to go somewhere in a car, try to hook
up with other people going the same place.
Carpooling like this helps cut the number of
cars on the road, reducing air pollution.
Encourage your parents and friends to
follow your example of walking, bicycling,
or carpooling.

21

Cleaner Air for the Future

The problem of air pollution will not be solved quickly. Pollutants dumped into the air a hundred years ago are still floating around today. That's even more reason to do what we can now to cut down on activities that cause air pollution. In this way, we can begin to clean up our air and make our Earth a better place for the future.

More Books to Read

Air by Terry Jennings (Childrens Press)
Air Ecology by Jennifer Cochrane (Franklin Watts)
Pollution by Geraldine Woods and Harold Woods (Franklin Watts)

Places to Write

Here are some places you can write to for more information about air pollution. Be sure to tell them exactly what you want to know about. Give them your full name and address so that they can write back to you.

National Center for
    Atmospheric Research
Information and Education
    Outreach Program
P.O. Box 3000
Boulder, Colorado   80307-3000

Environment Canada
Inquiry Center
351 St. Joseph Boulevard
Hull, Quebec   K1A 0H3

Glossary

atmosphere (AT-muh-sfear): the gases that surround the Earth.

carbon dioxide: a gas in the Earth's atmosphere that contains one atom of carbon and two atoms of oxygen.

carbon monoxide: a colorless, odorless gas released when fossil fuels are burned; breathing carbon monoxide can cause death.

carpooling: sharing a ride with other people who are going to the same place.

catalytic converter: a device on a car that helps remove some dangerous gases from car exhaust.

chlorofluorocarbon (klore-oh-floor-oh-KAHR-buhn): a chemical that destroys the ozone layer; CFCs are found in refrigerator and air-conditioner coolant and plastic-foam containers.

environment (en-VIE-run-ment): the natural and artificial things that make up the Earth.

fossil fuels: coal, oil, natural gas, and gasoline; these fuels formed from decaying plant and animal remains buried beneath the Earth's surface millions of years ago.

hydrocarbon (hie-droh-KAHR-buhn): a chemical made up of hydrogen and carbon; hydrocarbons combine with other gases in the air to form a yellow or brown haze.

nitrogen dioxide: a gas made up of one atom of nitrogen and two atoms of oxygen; it forms a brown haze in the air.

scrubbers: devices that clean sulfur and other pollutants out of factory smoke before the smoke is released into the air.

sulfur (SUHL-fuhr): a chemical element that, in its gaseous state, contributes to air pollution.

Index